LEON KIRCHNER

DUO No. 2
for violin and piano

*Commissioned by Richard and Judith Hurtig and Viola and Richard Morse
in memory of Felix Galimir*

*The first performance was given by Ida Levin and Jeremy Denk
on 27 July 2002 at the Marlboro Music Festival, Marlboro, Vermont.*

duration ca. 14 minutes

AMP 8200
First Printing: December 2005

ISBN 0-634-09321-5

Associated Music Publishers, Inc.

DISTRIBUTED BY

HAL•LEONARD®
CORPORATION
7777 W. BLUEMOUND RD. P.O. BOX 13819 MILWAUKEE, WI 53213

for Felix Galimir

DUO No. 2 FOR VIOLIN AND PIANO

Leon Kirchner

LEON KIRCHNER

DUO No. 2
for violin and piano

violin

AMP 8200
First Printing: December 2005

ISBN 0-634-09321-5

Associated Music Publishers, Inc.

DISTRIBUTED BY

HAL•LEONARD®
CORPORATION
7777 W. BLUEMOUND RD. P.O. BOX 13819 MILWAUKEE, WI 53213

Violin

for Felix Galimir
DUO No. 2 FOR VIOLIN AND PIANO

Leon Kirchner

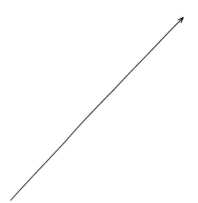